31
verses

LOVE

every
teenager
should
know

NEW HOPE®
PUBLISHERS
Imprint of Iron Stream Media
Birmingham, Alabama

Other books in the
31 Verses Every Teenager Should Know series:

Identity	*Inhabit*	*Character*	*Prime*
Rooted	*Sequence*	*Community*	*Reverb*
The Way	*Christ*	*Linked*	

New Hope® Publishers
100 Missionary Ridge
Birmingham, AL 35242
NewHopePublishers.com
An Imprint of Iron Stream Media
IronStreamMedia.com

New Hope Publishers serves its authors as they express their views, which may not express the views of the publisher.

Library of Congress Cataloging-in-Publication Data has been filed.

ISBN-13: 978-1-56309-275-6
Ebook ISBN: 978-1-56309-276-3

1 2 3 4 5—23 22 21 20 19

Contents

A Loaded Word

Love. This little word is loaded with baggage. Tons of it. And it's bursting at the seams. You've collected some souvenirs and scars from past experiences with love. Each day you wade through the messages that flood your media-saturated landscape. Most of us have either unrealistic fantasies of Hollywood romance or utter disillusionment with the very idea of love. No matter who you are, where you live, or what you do, you deal with love.

This book will not talk about romantic love. It won't deal with exaggerated expressions of personal preference. This book will talk about life, significance, and joy. This book will steer you toward a much better book, your Bible. See, the Bible is jam-packed with true stories, songs, and promises kept. Love is a common thread running throughout the pages of Scripture, a major theme since the beginning of time. God is the expert on love; this book is your crash course.

Even though we've probably never met, I'm excited you've decided to start this journey through this book and through your life. Love is what both are about, really. A life of love isn't easy, but I promise it'll be worth everything you put into it. God has spoken amazing things in these thirty-one verses we'll discuss. You'll grow a little with each step you take. Some will be bigger than others. Some may seem obvious. There may even be a leap of faith or two. But every step will get you moving in the right direction. God's love is more than you could ever anticipate. So hang on.

How to Use This Book

Now that you own this incredible little book, you may be wondering, "What do I do with it?"

Glad you asked. The great thing about this book is you can use it just about any way you want.

It's not a system. It's a resource that can be used in ways that are as unique and varied as you are.

A few suggestions . . .

The One-Month Plan
On this plan, you'll read one devotional each day for a month. This is a great way to immerse yourself in the Bible for a monthlong period. (Okay, we realize every month doesn't have thirty-one days. But twenty-eight or thirty is close enough to thirty-one, right?) The idea is to cover a lot of information in a short amount of time.

The Scripture Memory Plan
The idea behind this plan is to memorize the verse for each day's devotional; you don't move on to the next devotional until you've memorized the Scripture you're on. If you're like most people, this might take you more than one day per devotional. So this plan takes a slower approach.

The "I'm No William Shakespeare" Plan

Don't like to write or journal? This plan is for you. Listen, not everyone expresses themselves the same way. If you don't like to express yourself through writing, that's okay. Simply read the devotional for each verse, then read the questions. Think about them. Pray through them. But don't feel as if you have to journal if you don't want to.

The Strength in Numbers Plan

God designed humans for interaction. We're social creatures. How cool would it be if you could go through *Love* with your friends? Get a group of friends together. Consider agreeing to read five verses each week, then meeting to talk about them.

Pretty simple, right? Choose a plan. Or make up your own. But get started already. What are you waiting for?

Verse 1

"What no eye has seen, what no ear has heard, and what no human mind has conceived"—the things God has prepared for those who love him.

—1 Corinthians 2:9

One of the best parts of going to the movies is the previews. You know how it works—that guy with the deep, gravelly voice starts off with "In a world . . ." Then for about two-and-a-half minutes things explode, music intensifies, plot details emerge, and finally you hear a closing line like, "Coming soon . . . the adventure of a lifetime!" While the preview may look awesome, the movie is usually a mildly entertaining diversion rather than the adventure you were hoping for.

Too many people end up experiencing life the same way they do most movies. It starts off with great promise but turns out to be unsatisfying. Sure there were some good parts, but it could have been so much more. How can we experience the adventure that life is supposed to be?

Check out 1 Corinthians 2:6–9. Corinth was a popular place, full of rich and successful people. But many soon realized that the world's promises didn't deliver the life they hoped for; actually, things were getting pretty bad. In verse 9, the Apostle Paul wrote that loving God leads to a life greater than anything we can imagine. How can we tell this isn't just more hype?

Look back at verses 6 through 8. Paul said when we love Christ above everything else, we gain a new perspective that changes everything. The wisdom of God isn't head knowledge from a textbook; it's something you experience through the power of His Holy Spirit living inside you. You become a new person. You see things differently, hear God calling you to step out in faith, and trust that He's got you when you jump. That's the adventure of a lifetime—a life and love that your eyes, ears, and mind can't even comprehend.

Why do you think so many people seem so unsatisfied with their lives?

_____

_____

_____

Verse 6 says the wisdom and rulers of this age are "coming to nothing." What does that mean? What is the fatal flaw in following the world's promises?

_____

_____

_____

The adventure God has prepared for you hinges on whether you respond to Him in love. So how are you loving God with your life? Be honest with yourself, and avoid cliché answers.

_____

_____

_____

Verse 2

"Though the mountains be shaken and the hills be removed, yet my unfailing love for you will not be shaken nor my covenant of peace be removed," says the LORD, who has compassion on you.

—Isaiah 54:10

Who was your best friend in second grade? Who was the first super-athlete you can remember? What was your favorite TV show when you were ten? Your answers to these questions today would probably be different from what they were back then (though these memories may still hold great sentimental value). Ever wonder why things change so much? Sometimes change is for the better; other times it's disappointing. Occasionally it's hurtful, but mostly it's just different. Change is woven into the fabric of being a teenager. Your voice changes, your body changes, your likes and dislikes change. It may seem as though everything changes. Do you ever have moments when you wish something . . . anything . . . in your life were constant?

Read Isaiah 54:9–10. Here, God reassures His people of His love. The prophet Isaiah had the "fun" job of telling God's people about the serious consequences of their sin. The result was time spent in exile from their native land. (I can almost guarantee that Isaiah's best friend from second grade wasn't hanging out with him after that!) But then Isaiah got to share some great news. God chose to renew His covenant promise with the Israelites, telling them that His love would remain longer than the mountains that populated the countryside.

So what does this mean to us thousands of years later? The mountains are still there, right? The promise God gave to the Israelites, He also gives to us. In a world that may seem to spin out of control, God is right there. Though we may experience difficult times, His peace never leaves us. Though everything around us may seem as though it's falling apart, God's love and faithfulness never change. He won't move, retire, get replaced, or become outdated or outgrown. Nothing changes God's love. Nothing. Following Him doesn't guarantee an easy life, but His peace and love will never fail us.

What are some events in your life that have shaken you? How did God help you through these situations?

_____

_____

_____

How will you help others know God's unfailing and unchanging love?

_____

_____

_____

God revealed His love for Israel even through discipline. How has God shown His love for you through discipline, and what lasting difference did it make?

_____

_____

_____

Verse 3

Whoever does not love does not know God, because God is love.

—1 John 4:8

Rick Hoyt has competed in more than one thousand races, including six Iron Man competitions. He has biked and run across the entire US in only 45 days. But more amazing is the fact Rick cannot walk or talk because of an accident during his birth. He got into racing by telling his dad, with the help of a computer, that he wanted to run a five-mile benefit race. But just because he wanted to, that didn't mean he could. The only way Rick could compete in any of these races was with the help of his father, Dick Hoyt. His father pushes him in a wheelchair when he runs, pulls him when he swims, and carries him in a special cart on the front of his bike.

Read 1 John 4:7–8. The Apostle John wrote this book to all believers, encouraging them to not just talk about Jesus but to live like Him. Having known Jesus personally when He walked the earth, John realized Christ lived and loved perfectly, unlike anyone else in history. In these verses, he gave the facts of what knowing Jesus and being born into God's family meant: love. John saw firsthand the love of God in action, and he realized something so beautiful and pure could only be possible when God is working through us.

In the same way Rick realized that he couldn't run a race without his father, we must realize we can't truly love without our heavenly Father. Sure we sort of love, but not the way God intends. Our love is weak and usually selfish in nature. We tend to love when it's easy or when it benefits us. The love of God is unconditional, perfect, and impossible for us without Christ. We gain the ability to love through our relationship with God.

What have you experienced that would have been impossible in your own ability? (You explored underwater with scuba gear, a friend got you backstage or on the sidelines, etc.) How did the fact you couldn't have done it on your own change your appreciation of the experience?

_____

_____

_____

_____

Think of some instances where you truly felt God's love in your life. Describe the situation and how it made you feel.

_____

_____

_____

_____

According to 1 John 4:8, what is necessary for you to love fully? Can people see that in your life?

_____

_____

_____

_____

Verse 4

This is how God showed his love among us: He sent
his one and only Son into the world that we might
live through him.

—1 John 4:9

Everyone remembers Dr. Seuss's classic holiday tale, *How
the Grinch Stole Christmas*. Yeah, the book and subsequent
movies were intended for children, but it's a classic, and it con-
tains a truth we often forget. The Grinch was unable to love in
any way because his heart was "two sizes too small." All he
knew was bitterness and selfishness. So the Grinch disguised
himself as Santa Clause, sneaked down to the the local village,
and stole everyone's Christmas presents. After a night of loot-
ing, the Grinch traveled to the top of a mountain, intending to
dump the items over and into an abyss. He seemed to revel in
the thought of the pain he would cause. But to his surprise,
rather than tears and cries from the village he heard a joyous
Christmas song. That's when he realized, "Maybe Christmas,
perhaps, means a little bit more." And it changed him.

Read 1 John 4:9–10. This is believed to be one of the
last New Testament books written. Its elderly author had a
story similar to Dr. Seuss's beloved villain. He wasn't shaggy
and green, but before meeting God's Son, John once had a

7

reputation for his passion and, some say, a fiery temper (Luke 9:54). He and his brother were called the "Sons of Thunder" (Mark 3:17). But meeting someone who loved him no matter what changed this disciple. John became known as the apostle of love. He spent most of his life proclaiming our need for God and letting His love give us new life.

Similar to the Grinch, without Christ, we have hearts of stone, incapable of love. It's only when we realize that God loves us anyway that we can start to love the way He created us to. While we were unlovable enemies of God, His Son pursued us, never giving up. Our hearts are shriveled with sin until He transforms us. When we see the love of God in Jesus and turn from our selfish ways, our old natures are replaced with His life. This unconditional love hasn't given up on us. Our hearts can be radically changed, and life will never look the same.

Describe your heart. Is it calloused or small, full of anger or selfishness? Is it capable of loving, forgiving, and believing?

_____

_____

_____

Can you wrap your brain around the King of all kings being in love with you and pursuing you? What change has resulted from this love?

_____

_____

_____

In response to His loving you first, what are some practical ways you will love others today?

_____

_____

_____

Verse 5

To love him with all your heart, with all your under-standing and with all your strength, and to love your neighbor as yourself is more important than all burnt offerings and sacrifices.

—Mark 12:33

Have you ever played a game called hot/cold? Here's how you play. You hide something, and as someone else looks for it, you give clues by saying "warm" or "hot" as they get closer to it and "cool" or "cold" as they get farther away.

In Mark 12:28–34, Jesus played a game of hot/cold with a teacher of the Law. The teacher recognized Jesus' exceptional knowledge of Scripture, so he posed a challenging question as a test: "What's the most important command?" Jesus gave a two-part answer to the single question: "Love God and love your neighbor as yourself." Read verses 33–34 again. Notice how much this impressed the teacher of the Law. Jesus then responded as though to say, "You're getting warmer." The Lord's motivation was not to give this guy a hard time, nor was it to hide the truth from him. Jesus was trying to help him learn a very important lesson—love is greater than religion.

While this may sound like a slight toward religion, it's really not. Jesus wanted to help this man—and us today—see that religious habits, activities, and lifestyles are only as good as the love that motivates them. For example, what good is it to show up at a church building every week on a certain day at a particular time if our lives aren't filled with God's love? That would merely be another event in our busy schedules, an empty routine. Love, however, turns every minute of everything we do into something that brings God honor. Everywhere we go becomes a place of worship. Religion becomes relationship. When we begin to understand this truth, we're getting hot.

What did Jesus mean when He told this teacher he was not far from the kingdom of God? Looking at your life, how close or far are you from living a kingdom life?

_____

_____

_____

_____

Many religions teach similar morals and good deeds. What separates being a follower of Christ from being devoted to another religion?

_____

_____

_____

_____

How can you make sure your religious practices are actually acts of love in your relationship with Christ?

_____

_____

_____

_____

Verse 6

I do not hide your righteousness in my heart; I speak of your faithfulness and your saving help. I do not conceal your love and your faithfulness from the great assembly.

—Psalm 40:10

As of 2018, Apple Podcasts featured more than 500,000 active podcasts with more than 18.5 million episodes. Podcasts are a result of the easy Internet access people have today. You don't have to be famous. You don't have to be qualified by position or prestige. All you need is a computer, an opinion, and a hankering to share information, and you too can have a podcast. Podcasts provide people an outlet to express their personal feelings and thoughts. However, since podcasts are on the Internet, anybody can listen to them. So while podcasts are personal, they're by no means private.

The Book of Psalms, the worship manual for the Hebrew people, was somewhat like a podcast. In it David and the other writers expressed personal feelings of worship, petition, and thanksgiving to God. Their intimate expressions toward Him were not kept private. They were intended for use in public worship. Read Psalm 40:7–10. Notice the personal nature of verse 10. David had a desire to proclaim God's righteousness, faithfulness, salvation, and love before the masses. Remaining silent about his faith wasn't an option.

As followers of Christ, we have to adopt the same attitude. While our faith is internal and intimate, we cannot keep it to ourselves. If everyone considered their faith not for public consumption, who would tell others about Christ? Our faith has to be like a podcast—personal but also for the world to see. The cry of David's heart—proclaiming God's righteousness, faithfulness, salvation, and love before the world—must also be the passion of our lives. Our faith is most definitely personal, but by no means private.

What are some practical ways you can go public with a private matter like your faith in God?

_____

_____

You may have been raised in a family that taught you belief in God, or you may spend a lot of time with others who proclaim Jesus as their Lord and Savior. But what makes your faith personal? If you don't feel as though your faith is personal, what can you do to take greater ownership of it?

_____

_____

What are you passionate about? How can you express God's righteousness, faithfulness, salvation, and love to others through the things you're passionate about?

_____

_____

Verse 7

So be very careful to love the LORD your God.

—Joshua 23:11

Imagine a married couple who coincidentally shared the same birthday. Consider this scenario. One half of the couple begins thinking months in advance about the other's gift. He or she places phone calls, makes dinner reservations, and carefully chooses the perfect present. The other person starts thinking about a gift the night before. He or she makes a frantic dash to the drug store, chooses a cheesy card, and scribbles a birthday wish. Both members of the couple claim to love the other, but which one made it more evident? Obviously, the one who intentionally thought ahead and made a plan.

Our relationship with God can resemble this imaginary situation. How? Read Joshua 23:9–11.

In these verses Joshua gave his farewell address to the Hebrew people. Joshua took over for Moses as leader of the Israelites after they crossed into the Promised Land. Here, he reminded them of all God had done for them as they moved into the place He had prepared for them. God made His love for His people evident through His actions on their behalf. In verse 11 Joshua reminded the Hebrews that they must be intentional about their love for God.

In our world, we must also be extremely intentional in the way we express our love for God. We can be quick to profess a love for God, but what does the whole story of our lives say? Far too often our treatment of God more closely resembles that person giving a drug store birthday card at the last minute—doing the bare minimum, but not offering full-fledged devotion. In an unbelieving world, we make our love for God evident by being mindful of our witness and devotion to Him at all times.

What are some steps you can take to be more intentional in the ways you love God?

_____

_____

_____

_____

Have you ever been guilty of giving God the bare minimum? Most of us have. What makes you think this is an acceptable way to live your faith? What can you do to avoid this trap?

_____

_____

_____

_____

Being intentional carries great risk. What are some of these risks? What are the benefits to intentionally loving God with your whole life?

_____

_____

_____

_____

Verse 8

If I give all I possess to the poor and give over my body to hardship that I may boast, but do not have love, I gain nothing.

—1 Corinthians 13:3

Have you ever played Guitar Hero or Rock Band? If you have, you know how much fun they are. If you haven't, don't start now—the addiction level is off the charts. Save yourself while you can! Actually, there's a group of folks who really can't stand these games. You might ask, "Who doesn't love to jam like a rock star in the privacy of their living room?" Well, real musicians don't! They're afraid people will be satisfied playing music on fake instruments and never learn to play the real thing. They have a good point. It's much easier to memorize when to hit a button than to play a chord on a real guitar. Regardless, the hard truth is if you can't play a real instrument, you can't be in a real band.

As followers of Christ, there's one thing we need before we can do anything else. Read 1 Corinthians 13:1–3. The Apostle Paul taught the church at Corinth what it means to be a follower of Christ. The broader context of these verses is Paul's teaching on spiritual gifts. In verse 3, he reminded the Corinthians that no matter what gift you may have or how charitable you may be, unless you exercise gifts with love, they're null and void.

The same is true for us. It doesn't matter what gift we have or what we do; unless we do it with love, it's useless. Sound harsh? It's sort of like trying to be in a real band without knowing how to play an instrument. A person may look and act the part, but unless they can really play, they can't be a real rocker. Until we understand that love for God and others is the key to life, we won't be the people God wants us to be.

Why is an act of generosity not motivated by love useless? Doesn't the end justify the means?

_____

_____

_____

_____

Honestly, it's easy to look like a follower of Christ. How do you avoid being satisfied in just looking the part?

_____

_____

_____

_____

Most of the time Christ followers are known for what we don't do. How can you help redefine what it means to be a follower of Christ in our culture by being known for what you actually do? What are some things you can do to show the world you're all about love?

_____

_____

_____

_____

Verse 9

Love is patient, love is kind. It does not envy, it does not boast, it is not proud.

—1 Corinthians 13:4

I love Netflix."

"I love my boyfriend." (Or girlfriend.)

"I love freshly baked, homemade chocolate chip cookies and Blue Bell ice cream."

"I love playing football, soccer, basketball, and volleyball."

Have you ever stopped to think about how loosely we throw the word *love* around? What is love anyway? What do you really love?

Read 1 Corinthians 13:4–6. Paul had just spent a couple of years in Corinth establishing a church for the Gentiles. This city was the headquarters of trade and wealth. The gospel was foreign to most of this city because it was not presented elaborately, nor was it pleasing to most of their ears. When Paul left the city, trouble broke out in the church he had established. This letter was written to bring them back to the basics of how the church was meant to operate and to show them what real love looks like.

Just as the church in Corinth had to be reminded of how true love looked because they had a weak understanding of it, we to need to be reminded by this Scripture that loving is about much more than tasty sweets or favorite sports. So often we belittle love to being just an emotion or feeling. A right understanding of love is much more powerful than we give it credit for. The love described in these verses is patient and always seeking to benefit others. This kind of love can restore relationships that our human love might have already given up on. This love is powerful enough to lead people into a trusting relationship with Jesus Christ. God wants our love to reflect His and to be patient, kind, humble, and polite.

What are some ways you use the word *love* loosely?

_____

_____

_____

_____

What do you think would happen if your love started to look like the love described in these verses?

_____

_____

_____

_____

Do you have any relationships that need this kind of love? Write down the names of these people, and begin praying that God will help you love them the way He describes in His Word.

_____

_____

_____

_____

Verse 10

Love must be sincere. Hate what is evil; cling to what is good.

—Romans 12:9

Have you ever seen Criss Angel or David Blaine on television? They're both highly skilled illusionists. We watch with pure amazement as they perform all sorts of ridiculous stunts. It's easy to get lost in the production for a moment and believe that what you see is reality. But these guys, and other magicians, are skilled at grand illusions. They create seemingly impossible situations and suspend our disbelief, even if momentarily.

Read Romans 12:9–10. The Book of Romans is known as one of the most powerful documents ever written. Paul wrote this book to the church in Rome. He wanted to solidify the truth that they believed. This book answers so many questions that it seems to cover every major component of our faith. Paul's motive was to make sure the Romans were established in genuine belief in God and Christ. He knew the supreme importance of love and wanted to demonstrate how real love plays out.

Love is one of the few instances where grand illusion has no effect. In most cases there's no faking it when it comes to love. No smoke or perfect angle can make unreal love look genuine. To be firm in your beliefs, love must be the foundation upon which everything else is built. Without love our faith in Christ is nothing more than a bad magic trick where we're the only ones being fooled. Sincere love puts others above ourselves and doesn't require an audience or a pat on the back. Real love is an outpouring of God on everyone we come in contact with.

Sometimes it's easy to be caught up in the "magic show" of appearing to live faithfuly in Christ. Are there areas in your life where you need the Lord to make your love more real? What are they?

_____

_____

_____

_____

Why is it important for your love to be sincere?

_____

_____

_____

_____

Have you ever been loved insincerely? How did you feel?

_____

_____

_____

_____

How can you be sure your love is sincere?

_____

_____

_____

_____

Verse 11

Jesus replied, "Anyone who loves me will obey my teaching. My Father will love them, and we will come to them and make our home with them."

—John 14:23

Imagine it's Friday night, and the final installment of your favorite franchise has just come out. You've been in suspense for months. Your friends are going, and all that's keeping you from purchasing your ticket is getting your parents' approval. Their answer is a disappointing no. The reason they give is, "Because I said so." Wouldn't it be great if there were a better reason than, "Because I said so"?

Read John 14:23–29. John was writing this book as an old man, remembering his three-and-a-half years with Jesus. His main focus was declaring Jesus as the Messiah and the Son of God. This particular chapter records a conversation between Jesus and His disciples concerning Him being crucified and leaving them. We see Jesus comforting His friends and explaining that what was about to happen was the will of God. He also said He would be with them during the trials to come, and He would prepare a place for them to be reunited in heaven.

The Bible teaches us to be obedient to our parents and to God whether we understand it or not. Even though we should be willing to obey God simply because He said so, He loves us enough to tell us why. Scripture says that if we really love God, we'll be obedient to His commands. Because of this, His Spirit will come and make His home with us. When we love God, obedience is a beautiful thing. Obedience becomes satisfying because it keeps us in God's presence. Now, instead of a list of do's and don'ts, His teachings become a description of holiness and relationship with Christ. Instead of a bunch of rules, the Bible becomes a conversation about life.

Are there times when following God seems to be a bunch of do's and don'ts?

_____

_____

_____

Is your motivation in obeying God because He says so or because you know He loves you and you want to be in His presence?

_____

_____

_____

How does knowing that following His rules keeps you close to Him change the way you look at obedience?

_____

_____

_____

Do some soul-searching. Ask the Lord to reveal your motivation for keeping His commands. If you realize it's because someone has told you to, pray He will begin to make His joy and presence come alive in your heart.

_____

_____

_____

Verse 12

No one has ever seen God; but if we love one another, God lives in us and his love is made complete in us.

—1 John 4:12

A lot of people live by the motto, "I'll believe it when I see it." This seems reasonable, but there are some real consequences to that kind of thinking. If you have to literally see something before you'll believe it, then you can no longer believe in wind, gravity, heat, oxygen, anyone without a photograph or painting of their likeness, photosynthesis, earthquakes, love . . . you get the idea. While you can't physically see these things, you can see the evidence of them. The same is true for our relationship with Christ. Since the world can't actually see Jesus walking around, calming storms, turning water into wine, you know . . . doing Jesus stuff, how can they know He's real?

Read 1 John 4:12–15. The Apostle John wrote this letter to help people understand that Jesus actually came in the flesh, died, and rose again. He wasn't just a religious ideal or spiritual illusion; He was a real person. John wanted his readers to understand how the real power of Jesus' Resurrection is evident to the world when His followers love others just as He loved them.

Today, God has entrusted His message of love to us. It's our responsibility to share this message with the world. Fortunately, we don't have to do this alone. Every Christ follower is called to this task, but even better than that, we also have God's Holy Spirit as our helper. So while Jesus doesn't physically hang out at the local Starbucks chatting people up about the kingdom of God, He is spiritually present with people who don't yet know Him, through us. We make the invisible God visible. Just like gravity or an earthquake, the evidence (our lives) proves the strength of His love. Others can believe, even though they can't literally see Jesus, because they see Him in us.

How would you rate yourself on the way you love others? How do you love your family? People who hurt you? Those who are unlovely?

_____

_____

_____

_____

What can you do to constantly remind yourself that you're God's representative of love here on earth? How would being more mindful of this truth change the way you live?

_____

_____

_____

_____

How would your school, youth group, or cluster of friends change if you took a stand for love? What would your life look like?

_____

_____

_____

_____

Verse 13

We love because he first loved us.

—1 John 4:19

Remember the note? Four little words: "Do you like me?" with two check boxes labeled *yes* and *no*. Or maybe instead of a note, a friend came to you on someone else's behalf to ask if you liked them. Or maybe you received a text. Whichever way, the answer changed everything. The drama and suspense swirling around this lingering question was mind-numbing; it could spread throughout your entire circle of friends and beyond. Even if you didn't previously know that the person who liked you existed, simply discovering they were interested in you was huge. Be honest. You saw the world differently. It gave you confidence, changing your attitude and therefore your actions. You were more thoughtful about what you would wear, say, and do (and how you would smell).

With this in mind, read 1 John 4:19–20. John wrote this letter explaining what it meant to be in a relationship with God. He described love and went over how people would act if they were truly in love with God, going into a lover-versus-hater thing. Here, John relayed the message—God loved you first. This news should motivate a response. Verse 20 goes on to say that seeing who loves God back is as simple as reading a check box.

Before God took the first step, initiating contact with us through His written Word (Scripture), His friends (prophets), and ultimately Himself (Jesus), we didn't give God a second thought. The Bible says we weren't looking for God; we were actually His enemies before Christ came to us. He stepped out to make His love known, inviting us into relationship with Him. That changed everything. Knowing we're loved should change our attitude and actions. Now we can love Him in return, and this mysterious love is so contagious it should spread throughout our entire sphere of influence. Does it? Yes or no?

How have you responded to the news that God wants a relationship with you? Has it changed anything about you?

_____

_____

_____

Whom do you love, and what's your motivation for loving them?

_____

_____

_____

What difference does it makes when you love people because God loved you first? How will you spread the love?

_____

_____

_____

Write down the name of anyone you can think of to take the first step with and find out what they know about the love of Christ. Pray for motivation to invite them into a relationship with God.

_____

_____

_____

Verse 14

By this everyone will know that you are my disciples, if you love one another.

—John 13:35

What comes to mind when you hear the name Michael
Phelps? The world's fastest swimmer? Twenty-three
gold medals? Ate 12,000 calories a day during the Olympics?
Michael Phelps has a lifestyle and habits that set him apart
from everyone around him. His sacrifices have proven worth
it. He has earned a reputation for an uncommon ability. Sure,
as a person, he's much more than a swimmer; but for most
people, his Olympic triumphs define him. So what dominates
and defines your life? How are you known?

Check out what Jesus said about our identities and repu-
tations in John 13:34–35. Here, Jesus was spending some final
moments with the disciples before His death. They didn't
know the Cross was coming, but He did, so Christ spoke pas-
sionately about what was most important in life. In verse 35,
Jesus made things simple. There is something worth being so
devoted to that your devotion becomes obvious to everyone.

As followers of Christ, we should be defined as people
with an uncommon ability—loving each other as Christ
loves us. This is not just for our sake; it's for His. While we
might be labeled athlete, nerd, hipster, prep, or some other

tag someone slaps on us, how we love each other will earn a reputation. This is what will set us apart to the rest of the world as Jesus' followers. It's a lot easier to depend on church activities, T-shirts, religious music, or whatever else to set us apart. But how we love others is the greatest indicator of our devotion to Christ. Are we satisfied with being labeled by the stuff we're into, what we own, how we dress . . . or could we really be known for loving just as Christ does?

How do you think people see you? How do you wish they saw you? How can you change the way people see you?

_____

_____

_____

_____

What can you do to avoid defining people simply by what they've done? What's the danger in labeling someone only according to what they may have done?

_____

_____

_____

_____

It's super easy to judge a book by its cover. How do you move beyond categorizing people to loving them?

_____

_____

_____

_____ _____

Verse 15

Be completely humble and gentle; be patient, bearing with one another in love.

—Ephesians 4:2

It was the game that would decide who went to the college softball playoffs. Sara Tucholsky, a senior player for Western Oregon University, had just hit the first home run of her career. In her excitement, she forgot to touch first base. Turning back, she injured her knee and fell to the ground. Mallory Holtman, a player from Central Washington University who was her school's career leader, did the most selfless thing imaginable. The rules stated that if Sara's teammates touched her, in order to help her continue around the bases, she would have been out. So Mallory Holtman, along with teammate Liz Wallace, stooped down, picked Sara up, and helped her opponent around every base, literally carrying her to her home run.

Read Ephesians 4:1–6. The chapters leading up to these verses describe the spiritual blessings received through Jesus Christ. This letter opens our eyes to the riches we inherit as part of God's family, contrasting them with the dullness and filthiness He came to save us from. In chapters 4 through 6, Paul began to apply these riches to a way of life. He wanted all believers to begin humbly running the race of righteousness, drawn together by their shared purpose.

Ultimately, we're all on the same team. In one moment the Western Oregon and Central Washington teams were literally unified by a common goal. Winning lost its luster in comparison to the richness of doing what was right. Love won the game. Christ wants the same for us. It no longer matters who's right or wrong, or who wins or loses, but that we reflect the attitude of Christ and lift one another up in love. Humility requires sacrifice, but when we honor God with this attitude, He's able to do amazing things through us. Godly attitudes display Christ's love to the world.

In your own words, describe what the attitude of Christ looks like.

_____

_____

_____

Where in your life do you lack humility, gentleness, patience, and love?

_____

_____

_____

What are some things you can do to begin letting go of pride and selfishness and picking up the attitude of Christ instead?

_____

_____

_____

In what ways do you think Christ's attitude will benefit you and help you create an environment of unity?

_____

_____

_____

Verse 16

Anyone who loves their father or mother more than me is not worthy of me; anyone who loves their son or daughter more than me is not worthy of me.

—Matthew 10:37

In Nepal, a country between India and China, it is difficult to share about Christ. Roughly 95 percent of the country is Hindu, Buddhist, or Muslim. Rajan grew up Hindu, but his life changed drastically when he encountered Jesus through one of only three Christ followers in his village. When he renounced his religion and embraced Christ, his family disowned him, his friends shunned him, and he was forced to leave his home and village. His Hindu neighbors dug up his cauliflower and potatoes, ruining a year's worth of income. Rajan lost everything for his relationship with Christ, but instead of discouraging him, it made Jesus more precious to him.

Read Matthew 10:37–39. Matthew, a tax collector, wrote this book to tell about Jesus' life, including His birth, ministry, death, and Resurrection. In this chapter, Jesus commissioned His disciples concerning the ministry they would have and the miracles they would do. He also told them about the suffering they would endure. But He told them not to fear because He would be with them and see them through it.

As followers of Christ, we're never told that our journey will be easy. Instead, we're told to be in the world and not of it, and that we'll face persecution. But life with Christ is worth any suffering we might face. This verse appears to be about not loving people, but really it's about loving God more than people. He has to be our first love, and if need be, the one that we choose over anyone or anything else. When we're in love with God, our love for family and friends actually increases, even if they persecute us. When we're willing to sacrifice everything for loving Him, it shows an unbelieving world just how valuable and worthy of belief He really is.

Can you imagine being in the situation like Rajan's, losing everything you have because you're a follower of Christ? What would you do in that situation?

_____

_____

_____

Does Jesus really mean this much to you? Is He the most important person in the universe to you?

_____

_____

_____

Suffering for Christ doesn't have to be as drastic as your family turning against you or being forced out of your town. It can be as simple as a friend making fun of you because of your beliefs or morals. What are some everyday examples of struggles you might face (or have already faced)?

_____

_____

_____

Verse 17

Greater love has no one than this: to lay down one's life for one's friends.

—John 15:13

Brittany, an average girl who doesn't get much attention, shuffles through the lunch line at school. She and her best friend Kristen normally eat by themselves in the corner of the lunchroom. This day, however, is different. As Brittany carries her tray to her normal seat, Mallory, the coolest girl in school, calls her name, inviting her to sit with her and her friends. Everything in Brittany wants to join the popular group; this opportunity may never come again. She glances at Kristen sitting at the table by herself, takes a deep breath, and with a smile, tells Mallory she already has lunch plans.

Read John 15:11–13. These were Jesus' last hours before the Cross. He'd just finished the Last Supper with His disciples, left the table, and started walking to the garden of Gethsemane. While walking with His friends, Jesus twice brought up the fullness of joy that came from remaining in His love and learning to love others the way He loved them. In verse 13 Jesus described the most complete expression of love. He explained He would be laying down His life—literally dying—for His friends (including us).

There's no greater way to love than to lay down our lives for our friends. It's easy to overcomplicate this, turning it into what-if scenarios of life or death, but most simply it means putting our friends before ourselves. Before we worry about dying for someone, we should ask ourselves if we're even willing to live for anyone else. Denying ourselves and putting other people's interests before our own are evidence of the most powerful form of love that exists. This expression of love leaves us so satisfied that we'll start seeking opportunities to serve others more often.

Describe what you would do if you were in Brittany's position.

_____

_____

_____

What would your friends say about you? Are you loving them or loving yourself?

_____

_____

_____

Has anyone ever laid down their life for you in the sense that they put your interests before theirs? If so, how did this make you feel?

_____

_____

_____

What are some everyday examples of how you can lay down your life for your friends?

_____

_____

_____

Verse 18

The foreigner residing among you must be treated as your native-born. Love them as yourself, for you were foreigners in Egypt. I am the LORD your God.

—Leviticus 19:34

Have you ever seen *Indiana Jones and the Kingdom of the Crystal Skull*? It was a little strange but very biblical. *Huh?* You might be wondering if we watched the same movie. Let me explain. By the way—*spoiler alert!* Yes, it was about aliens, but it was also about being obedient to authority and treating others right. Seriously . . . think about it. The Crystal Skull told Indy to return it to its proper place. He did. The aliens also didn't like anyone trying to misuse the power of the skull to control others, so there were consequences. Okay, maybe it's a stretch, but stick with me.

The Bible actually provides specific instructions about how to treat foreigners, "aliens" in some translations. Really, in Leviticus 19:33–34. In the Book of Leviticus, God instructed His people about everything from what they should eat to how they should worship. Obviously, this passage is not about beings from another planet but about people from a foreign country living among the Israelites. God reminded the Hebrews of how poorly they were treated when they were foreigners in Egypt . . . so they were to treat others with the love and respect they wished that they had been shown at the time.

Bet you didn't expect Leviticus to be so relevant today. According to Pew Research Center, in 2018 more than 40 million people living in the United States were born in another country. Verse 34 says, "I am the LORD your God." (In other words, "I'm the authority you should listen to.") We have to love our neighbors as ourselves. Sound familiar? Jesus quoted it because people needed reminding (both then and now). Treating others with respect is a divine directive we cannot ignore. We can make no excuses or offer any attempts to justify prejudice. No crude jokes or leaving people out. Everyone, no matter where they were born, deserves equal respect.

Why do you think God felt it necessary to include teaching in His Word about people who are aliens?

_____

_____

_____

_____

Do you know people who are not native to this country? What can you do to make them feel more welcome? What can you do to show them God's love?

_____

_____

_____

_____

Passages like these show God's love and concern for all people. Write a prayer below asking God to give you a heart for all people.

_____

_____

_____

_____

Verse 19

Show proper respect to everyone, love the family
of believers, fear God, honor the emperor.

—1 Peter 2:17

In the 1980s (I know, ancient history), a song came out that resonated with teenagers. It was by a group called Twisted Sister (look them up; they're bizarre), and it was called "We're Not Gonna Take It." The defiant anthem basically told off anyone who might be an authority figure. Teachers? We're not going take it! Bosses? We're not going to take it! Parents? We're not going to take it . . . anymore!

This song might be fun to hear blaring over the loud speakers at a basketball game, but it has an inherent problem. Read 1 Peter 2:13–17. Wait. So the Bible tells us to live under the authority of others? We have to take it? Yes and yes. These verses were written to people who lived under a Roman authority that was not friendly to Christ followers. In verse 17, the Apostle Peter told his readers to show respect to everyone—even the pagan government. Why? Because like it or not, even the government is under God's authority.

At this point in your life, you probably want to turn the page and forget these verses, but it's important you don't. God set certain people and systems in place to help guide us through life. Nobody hates guardrails on a treacherous mountain road.

Those rails are a good analogy of what authority figures are today: support, protection, and for our best interest. Our lives can be pretty treacherous right now. Besides, if we can't submit to the authority of those over us on earth, how do we expect to submit to God? He's the ultimate authority in our lives, but that doesn't dismiss other authorities. He put them in place. Plus, showing respect gives greater credibility to what we say about God. Respect His authority, but respect others too.

Who are the authority figures in your life? Do you have trouble submitting to them? What are some ways you can let God help you submit to authority?

_____

_____

_____

_____

Look back at verse 17. Why do you think God wants us to love other believers? What does it mean to fear God? Why do you think God wants us to honor the emperor?

_____

_____

_____

_____

Does it give you comfort or make you feel controlled to know God has ultimate authority over your life? Why?

_____

_____

_____

_____

Verse 20

But I tell you, love your enemies and pray for those who persecute you.

—Matthew 5:44

Several years ago, Apple ran a series of commercials called "Get a Mac." From an advertising perspective, they were genius (no Apple store pun intended). It featured a young, easygoing Mac guy teasing an uptight, dumpy PC guy. Microsoft eventually launched their own TV ads, firing back with how cool and diverse their users actually are (attempting to point Apple's negative stereotypes back on them). The commercials were fairly tame, but the rivalry is real. They're essentially political smear campaigns, but humorous. In the computing world, Mac and PC are sworn enemies.

Read Matthew 5:43–48. These verses are part of Jesus' Sermon on the Mount where the heart of a Christ follower's ethics is found. Here, Jesus spoke very clearly about how His followers were to live, addressing wealth, marriage, murder, prayer, and more. Christ even explained how His followers should treat their enemies. He plainly stated His thoughts in verse 44. Read it again. Wow.

Just about everybody has a situation in life where someone becomes their enemy. We may not be caught up in a computer powerhouse rivalry. Our rivalry might be with a person fighting for the same scholarship we are. Or maybe with the people who bully us. Perhaps it's with the players from a rival team. Whether it's someone who seriously annoys us or someone who causes actual pain and suffering, an enemy can result from any number of situations. In each situation, regardless of how intense it may be, Jesus says love is not optional but expected. It's not one choice among many or an option reserved for the holiest of holy people; love is it. If we claim to belong to Christ . . . if we say He is our Lord . . . if we call Him Savior . . . as hard as it may be, we have to love our enemies. And not just love them, but pray for them as well.

Do you have any enemies? Why are they your enemies? If you don't have enemies, do your friends have them? How can you help bring them together?

Why wouldn't God just want you to ignore your enemies? Wouldn't that be easier? Why would He want you to go so far as to pray for them?

Praying for people means you want their well-being. List some people whom you may have an issue with or who may have issue with you. Ask God to help you love them. Then pray for their well-being.

Verse 21

Do not seek revenge or bear a grudge against anyone among your people, but love your neighbor as yourself. I am the LORD.

—Leviticus 19:18

In the 1950s, Jim Elliot, Nate Saint, and three other men went to Ecuador to spread the gospel to an unreached tribe. When the group thought it was safe, they attempted to enter the Amazon jungle to meet the tribe face to face. On January 8, 1956, all five men were murdered by the very people they went to share the gospel with. Jim's wife and Nate's sister began learning the tribe's language and culture, and two years after their husband's and brother's deaths, went to live with the tribe. The love and forgiveness these women showed began to soften the tribe's angry hearts and created an opportunity for the greatest story of forgiveness, Christ's death on a Cross, to be shared. Many of the tribe came to know the Lord.

Read Leviticus 19:18. Leviticus can often be a confusing book to read. It's a list of laws the Lord gave to Moses concerning offerings, ceremonies, and priestly duties. These laws were intended to distinguish His people from the world and lead them in a holy life. The word *holiness* comes from the same root as the word *wholeness*. God wants His people to be whole, complete, and lacking nothing.

Usually when someone hurts us, our hearts desire revenge, even though God's Word tells us to forgive. This internal battle can leave us feeling broken and anything but complete. The Lord's plan is for us to be so whole in Him we're able to see the offense as an opportunity to show real love instead of bitter anger. When we forgive as God forgave us, we share the story of God's forgiveness with our offenders, and it frees us from pains we can't get rid of on our own.

Has anyone hurt you that you have not forgiven? If so, why are you holding on to that hurt?

_____

_____

_____

_____

Name those people and begin praying for your heart to heal. Pray the Lord will go before you and that His plan will be done instead of yours.

_____

_____

_____

_____

You must forgive in the same way God forgives you of your offenses to Him. Take a moment to thank the Lord for the forgiveness He so graciously gives you.

_____

_____

_____

_____

Verse 22

If your brother or sister is distressed because of what
you eat, you are no longer acting in love. Do not by
your eating destroy someone for whom Christ died.

—Romans 14:15

Skittles. Oh, the bliss of that sweet little bag of rainbow-flavored goodness. Whether you eat them by the color or by the handful, you can't go wrong . . . unless you happen to be Michael Sheridan. An honor student and class vice president, this eighth grader was anything but a troublemaker. But Michael was drawn into a scandalous media frenzy when he was suspended and stripped of his class title for buying candy from a classmate. What would normally be a routine exchange became a covert operation busted up by school officials. A wellness policy declared candy contraband, but the classmate knowingly offered it to Michael anyway.

Read Romans 14:12–18. Paul was writing to Christ followers in the cultural center of the ancient world. He was specifically addressing a popular controversy but also providing a general rule-of-thumb. The believers in Rome had different opinions about whether it was appropriate to associate within, let alone eat something from, the city's market. Meat from the market was often "blessed" by a merchant's idol, so some people felt they were participating in false religions. Other believers with a Jewish background felt some of the meat was unclean regardless, even without pagan practices. Others thought, "It's just a delicious hunk of meat!" Paul's solution was that even if it was no big deal in the readers' opinion, they shouldn't eat the meat if it could cause problems.

This is about giving love and respect instead of demanding our rights. Whatever it is, if you think it could become a distraction or a temptation for someone else, you should skip it. Maybe you would enjoy a party or concert but your friend could get into trouble by justifying a tempting situation. Christ gave up everything for you (and for your friend too), so it shouldn't be a big deal to let go of this one thing for His sake and for theirs. Whatever it is, leave it alone if you love your friend at all.

Would you be willing to give something up that you have every right to enjoy, even for a little while, if it would help somebody else see Christ's love? Why or why not?

_____

_____

_____

Think about some things that people have different opinions on, things that aren't a big deal to you. What can you do in situations where those things become controversial?

_____

_____

_____

Pray for awareness of how your choices influence other people's spiritual lives and for the wisdom to live as an encouragement instead of a distraction.

_____

_____

_____

Verse 23

Flee the evil desires of youth and pursue righteousness, faith, love and peace, along with those who
call on the Lord out of a pure heart.

—2 Timothy 2:22

You've probably heard stories of popular entertainers who have escaped the "sex, drugs, and rock and roll" lifestyle after finding Jesus. They have powerful testimonies of Christ's life-changing power, but not all of us have such dramatic experiences. You may or may not struggle with "big" sins (though there's no difference in God's eyes). We all have things that aren't good for us that we naturally want to chase when we need to run from them instead. There's no need to live like a rock star or hit rock bottom before getting your life right.

Read 2 Timothy 2:22. While in a Roman prison, Paul wrote the books of 1 and 2 Timothy as letters to Timothy, the young protégé who would continue the ministry Paul spent his life establishing. Paul knew his own life would soon be over, so he was challenging Timothy to run the race of faith with excellence, boldness, and discipline. In his first letter, Paul was more concerned with the church, but this second letter was focused on the attitude and behavior of his close friend.

There's danger in thinking that following Christ means giving up an exciting life. In reality, life with Jesus is essential to true happiness, satisfaction, and meaning. All the world's experiences leave us empty and needing something else. Scripture says we should separate ourselves from our naturally selfish and indulgent mentality. The best way to avoid the dangerous traps and pitfalls in life's journey is to surround ourselves with the right people. Even Christ had a group that ran with Him. Do those around us lead us in the right direction, or are they headed down a dead end? If we find those who call on the name of the Lord for guidance, we'll save ourselves some painful U-turns.

What things in your life are impure and not pleasing to God?

_____

_____

_____

In what ways have you tried to rid yourself of these burdens so you can be more like Jesus?

_____

_____

_____

Look at your group of friends, and the older people in your life too. Who can take this journey with you, helping you stay in line with Christ's heart?

_____

_____

_____

Pray that God will help you pursue faith, love, and peace. Also pray that sharing Christ's love will become more exciting and fulfilling than any of your heart's impure desires.

_____

_____

_____

Verse 24

For where your treasure is, there your heart will be also.

—Matthew 6:21

Pirate stories are always about treasure. Of course the treasure sought is not always, well . . . actual treasure. A good example of this is the Pirates of the Caribbean films. While they're quirky and a little convoluted, they show how far people will go to get what they want most. For Elizabeth, it was the freedom she craved. For Captain Jack Sparrow, his treasure was his ship, the *Black Pearl*. For Will Turner, it was the affection of Elizabeth Swann. Each one stopped at nothing to get what his heart desired.

Jesus understood our human inclination toward what we treasure. Look what He taught the crowds that followed Him in Matthew 6:19–21. In this famous Scripture passage, Jesus laid out the values and principles of His kingdom. He did this at the beginning of His public ministry to lay the foundation from the start. Life is a matter of the heart. His followers had to know that their inner lives (their hearts' desires) were a greater concern than the public appearance of having it all together.

In verse 21, Jesus said your heart is with your treasure. So what do you treasure? Sports? Grades? Relationships? Things? A good way to check your heart is to look at where you spend your time and money. Does it honor God? If your treasure has nothing to do with Him, you have an idol. If your thing could honor God but you're using it in a way that doesn't, you still have a problem. God has to be number one because you're going to chase whatever you treasure. God doesn't want anything to come between you and Him. Stop at nothing. Make Him your heart's desire.

Where do you spend your time and money? Do you allow God to have a say about what you do with your time and how you use your cash?

_____

_____

_____

List your top five priorities. Be totally honest with yourself. Is God at the top of that list?

_____

_____

_____

List why or why not below. If He's not, how can you make Him number one?

_____

_____

_____

How do you make evident to others that your love for God is the treasure of your life?

_____

_____

_____

Verse 25

They loved human praise more than praise from God.

—John 12:43

The rules for the National Cheerleaders Association's dance competition clearly state cheerleaders must perform a routine they learn four days before the competition. Samantha's cheer coach illegally brought in an NCA staff member weeks in advance to teach the squad the dance before competition. Samantha loves God and knew cheating wasn't pleasing to Him, so she refused to attend practice the days they were learning the routine. Her coaches and squad were furious with her decision. Although it was a tough choice, the peace she found in doing what was right was worth far more than any blue ribbon.

Read John 12:42–43. The previous chapter concluded with the Pharisees (people with religious education and influence) saying Jesus was essentially a traitor. From that day on, they plotted Jesus' death. In chapter 12, the honor due to Jesus was restored. His feet were anointed with oil, palm branches waived as He was hailed a Savior, and the voice of God glorified Him. Though some religious leaders even believed in Jesus, they feared what the Pharisees might say about them, so they chose not to confess Him.

We want praise from those we love the most. Think about it. When we feel a desire for someone's praise, that shows who we want to accept us in a relationship. Honestly, on a pretty regular basis we probably value the opinions of the world more than what pleases God. We might resemble the religious leaders who wanted to follow Christ, but our desire to be accepted keeps us from doing so. Starting today, don't miss the satisfaction of pleasing the only One who really matters by settling for friends' approval or recognition from someone with influence. The burden we feel to be accepted by others weighs us down, but pleasing God is liberating and eternally rewarding.

Think about a time when you made an unpopular decision, knowing it was the right thing to do in God's eyes. What happened?

_____

_____

_____

What have you done that might compromise your testimony of faith in God in order to fit in with a certain person or group of people?

_____

_____

_____

Sometimes we try hard to be like others. But what are you doing to be like Jesus? Pray that God will help you choose to follow Jesus, even when it's not popular.

_____

_____

_____

Verse 26

Whoever who loves a quarrel loves sin; whoever builds a high gate invites destruction.

—Proverbs 17:19

Do you ever watch or listen to a talk show? One where people are yelling at each other, all talking at the same time, insisting they're right? Maybe you were just looking for some news or entertainment and ended up stressed out and in a terrible mood. My point is not to cast judgment on anyone on some show but to look at my own life with those shows in mind.

Read Proverbs 17:19. Proverbs was a collection of wise sayings, an ancient method for passing on things learned from experience. The overall theme is simple truths that lead to a peaceful and righteous life. Traditionally considered King Solomon's project, nobody knows exactly how many proverbs were originally his or collected from other people, but the Bible is clear that Solomon had incredible insight. This guy had it all, literally. Unprecedented wealth. Unrivaled power. Innumerable women. Unequalled wisdom (though it doesn't take a genius to know that a thousand wives and girlfriends is asking for trouble). After trying everything life had to offer, Solomon concluded that a life spent loving God is the only thing that's satisfying and meaningful.

Do you constantly find yourself in the middle of some drama? A wise man once said that people who live that way end up with serious problems. I'm not talking a little messed up or in a bad phase but rather headed for destruction. Loving yourself so much that you're always defensive or offensive will ruin your life; it builds walls. This pushes others out of your life and doesn't leave room for God either. Arguing a lot is evidence of pride. Pride is loving yourself more than anything else, thinking you deserve whatever you want. That's really what all sin boils down to. If you love sin, you don't love God, and it doesn't take a genius to know that's just asking for trouble.

Do you gossip, back talk, or throw a fit when you don't get your way? What does this say about your love of self, God, and others?

_____

_____

_____

In what environments do you find yourself most likely to argue or become prideful? What about that setting encourages that behavior in you?

_____

_____

_____

Pray for a peaceful attitude. Ask God to give you the ability to admit when you are wrong and to learn from others when they are right.

_____

_____

_____

Verse 27

Keep your lives free from the love of money and be content with what you have, because God has said, "Never will I leave you; never will I forsake you."

—Hebrews 13:5

Michelle Tolentino was born in a poverty-stricken, drug-infested community in the Philippines. She lived with sixteen of her relatives in a small home. A drug addict, Michelle's father abandoned the family, and Michelle became fatherless. Her family's anger began to burn against Michelle because she looked like her father. At age six, Michelle was sponsored by a family through Compassion International. Through this generosity she came to know her heavenly Father. Her sponsor family sent their money as well as their love to Michelle, and her brokenness was replaced with hope and a bright future.

Read Hebrews 13:5–8. This letter urged Jewish believers among a Greek culture to persevere in following Christ. Life was tough. Their Jewish friends and families rejected them for believing in Christ, but they also weren't a part of their surrounding Greek culture. Persecution and temptation to want someone else's life bombarded these believers on all sides. It must have seemed that anything would have been better than what they were experiencing. Nothing was comfortable or easy. But God promised that life with Him was ultimately greater than any religious tradition or pleasure of this world.

In Christ, God gave us everything we'll ever need, and He promises to always be with us. When we want what others have, we're saying that God is not enough. It's easy to start thinking that if we had more of this or if that were different, then life would be better. But this self-destructive mentality eats away at you like an addiction; nothing ever satisfies. The truth is God always takes care of His children. When we start to give instead of take and love instead of hate, we start to look like our heavenly Father. Hoping in our future starts to change our lives, regardless of what we're going through today.

In what ways are you trusting that God is supplying all your needs? How hard is it to trust Him? Why?

_____

_____

_____

Identify some things you could do without. Can you share these things with others?

_____

_____

_____

Name some times when you felt the blessing of giving instead of getting. Where do you think that joy comes from?

_____

_____

_____

Pray that God will open your eyes to how satisfying He is and give you contentment in what He has provided for you.

_____

_____

_____

Verse 28

If anyone has material possessions and sees a brother or sister in need but has no pity on them, how can the love of God be in that person?

—1 John 3:17

Several years ago, New England Patriots quarterback Tom Brady was seen walking the streets of New York wearing a Yankees hat. This caused an uproar in Boston where the Patriots play. Endorsing this rival city called his loyalty into question. Sure, Brady is a football player and the Yankees are a baseball team, but folks from Boston don't support anything from New York. Ironically, the Patriots would end up losing to New York in that year's Super Bowl. How could any true Bostonian betray this sense of brotherhood? As a representative of a greater community, it seemed inexcusable.

As Christ followers, we simply cannot do some things. Look at 1 John 3:16–17. The Apostle John wrote this letter to a group of people who needed to understand what it meant to love. One of the key ways John encouraged his readers to show their love for others was to provide for the material needs of those who were lacking. In verse 17 he went so far as to say that those who have the ability to take care of someone, but don't, should have their love for God questioned.

Though it's a trivial comparison, while it's inappropriate for New England's quarterback to wear the gear of any New York team, it's inexcusable for Christ followers who have plenty to sit idly, not helping those in need. God blesses us materially so we can be a blessing to others. If we're not blessing others, we should be questioned on several levels. First, we're not being faithful with what God has entrusted to us. Second, we're not considering others in our community. Finally, we're not displaying that God's love is inside of us. Claiming to be loyal to Jesus but having no concern for brothers and sisters in need isn't just poor taste—it's inexcusable.

How has God blessed you materially? How can you use what you have to be a blessing to those in need?

_____

_____

_____

So many people are driven by materialism. How can you take a stand for simplicity when it comes to things? How can you encourage your friends to do the same?

_____

_____

_____

Why do you think it's important to share with those in need? How does this show that the love of God is in us?

_____

_____

_____

Verse 29

Dear children, let us not love with words or speech
but with actions and in truth.

—1 John 3:18

In the second Harry Potter novel, *Harry Potter and the Chamber of Secrets*, readers were introduced to a new character. His name was Gilderoy Lockhart. He was the new Defense Against the Dark Arts professor at the wizarding school Hogwarts. But more than that, he was known as an adventuresome world traveler and had authored numerous books detailing his exploits. However, as the story progressed, he was revealed to be more of an inept bumbler than a dashing hero. In the end, he turned out to be nothing more than a con artist and not much of a wizard. He couldn't back up his lofty claims with actions.

Read 1 John 3:18–22. The Apostle John wrote this letter to a community of Christ followers who came from a Jewish background. Because of the religious tradition they were coming out of, this group was struggling to remain unified. To help them stay together, John wanted his readers to know love was the most important thing. The love that would sustain them couldn't be just words; it had to be put into action.

This is so important for us today. Go back and review verse 18. Sadly, for many people, Christ followers have developed a reputation for being all talk and no walk, more bark than bite. While this doesn't mean we need to be ferociously aggressive or in people's faces, it does mean we need to match our words with our actions. If we say Jesus loves everyone and we're His followers, we have to follow that up by doing something about it. This reinforces the truth that love is a verb. It's active, not passive. Love requires more than good intentions or motivations. Love calls for actions and not just talk. We must be a people of truth and love in action because the world is watching us very closely.

Why is love that's backed up with actions more effective than love that's simply offered in words? How do the two go hand in hand?

How do you show love to your family? Your friends? Those you come in contact with randomly, such as restaurant servers or people at stores? Those you don't get along with?

Why does the world need to see Christ followers love in both deed and words? What are some things you could do (individually and as a group) to show your community that Christ followers love with words and deeds?

Verse 30

For the Spirit God gave us does not make us timid,
but gives us power, love and self-discipline.

—2 Timothy 1:7

Many families have an unwritten rule: "We can say or do anything we want to each other, but if anyone else messes with us, it's on!" Have you ever witnessed this rule in action? Two brothers are rudely insulting each other, then someone else jumps in, and immediately the defenses go up. A couple of sisters are calling each other names with no problems, but someone else comments, and a fight breaks out. It's a common thing. Families can be blunt with each other then fierce in defense of one another. That's what the deep abiding love of family can do. It's secure. It's sustained over time. It's bold.

As far as we know, the Apostle Paul did not have any children. However, he did have a spiritual son in Timothy. Read 2 Timothy 1:3–7. Second Timothy was most likely Paul's last letter before he was martyred. Paul could often be quite blunt while speaking in love. Here, he wrote to encourage Timothy to be bold in sharing the faith his mother and grandmother taught him and Paul witnessed in him.

Verse 7 serves as a word of encouragement to us as well. As followers of Christ, we have to be bold. We take a stand on behalf of our heavenly Father and our brothers and sisters in Christ. It's also very important to heed Paul's admonition about how to do this. We cannot be timid, but we must act in love and self-discipline. We do have a spirit of power but not of domination and intimidation. A healthy balance exists with strength under control and confidence with respect. This is possible through the power of the Holy Spirit in us. His power is deep and abiding. It's secure. It's sustained over time. It's bold. Therefore, we have to be the same.

Why is it important to be bold about our faith? How can we be bold about our beliefs but not overbearing or domineering?

_____

_____

_____

_____

How can you be bold in the way you love God? Others? Yourself?

_____

_____

_____

_____

Think about how the Holy Spirit has worked in your life. Write about a time when you felt Him giving you boldness to do what He wanted you to do.

_____

_____

_____

_____

Verse 31

Do everything in love.

—1 Corinthians 16:14

In 1886, Karl Benz patented the first gas-powered automobile. Everything we know about cars today was built upon his invention. Since that date, one thing is for certain, cars then and cars today cannot effectively run without power. Sure, a car can be put in neutral and pushed, but it operates in the mode it was created for when it runs on fuel. Even the Bugatti Veyron, the world's fastest car, will sit motionless with an empty tank, completely useless and wasting its potential.

Check out 1 Corinthians 16:14. This first letter was written to the church at Corinth, which was the most problematic church in the New Testament. This resort city struggled with the battle between flesh and spirit. Paul emphasized both of these to show the problems with the flesh and that with the Holy Spirit we're equipped to fix those problems. This chapter recaps that everything should be done with love since love defines the life of a Christ follower.

Like an engine without fuel, a person without love is powerless. Coasting through life without love is a waste. Sure, you can push forward, but you're giving up your great potential and the purpose you were created for. You're missing out on the excitement of the ride too! You can't act in godly love just because you want to, though. You have to seek God and ask Him to fill you with the love you need to do His work. Knowing that gas exists does nothing for your car. Don't settle for simply knowing about God's love; let Him fill you up until His love is burning pure and bright, propelling you into action. That's what you were created for. It'll be quite a ride, so invite your friends to come along too. Have fun. Do everything in love. Everything.

As a Christ follower, why would anything you do without love be considered useless?

_____

_____

_____

Does serving or doing God's work ever seem to be a burden to you, as though you were pushing a car instead of driving it? If so, why do you think that is?

_____

_____

_____

What steps can you take to be mindful of God's love in everything you do?

_____

_____

_____

Pray God will fill you to the brim with His love. Ask Him to show you how powerful His love is. Ask that you will begin to let it fuel all you do to serve Him.

_____

_____

_____

Closing

Hey! What a trip.

So this is like one of those movies where you get to the end only to realize it doesn't wrap up all nice and neat. Not only is a sequel on the horizon, a whole new world has been introduced. The possibilities are endless.

So where do you go from here? What you choose to do with this love you've been given is up to you, but God is on the move. He's inviting you to continue down this trail He's blazing. It'll take you places you never imagined.

Hopefully, your eyes have been opened to a new way of seeing life. Since God's love changes everything, how did you change over the time it took to journey through this book? Have your thoughts, actions, and interactions with others been transformed?

Some people create; others achieve. Many sing about it, write about it, or talk about it. But what I really want to know is will you live it? Will you show love in all you do, sharing it freely? As you go, keep this thought with you—Christ said we should be known for one thing: love.

How to Become a Christian

You're not here by accident. God loves you. He wants you to have a personal relationship with Him through Jesus, His Son. There is just one thing that separates you from God. That one thing is sin.

The Bible describes sin in many ways. Most simply, sin is our failure to measure up to God's holiness and His righteous standards. We sin by things we do, choices we make, attitudes we show, and thoughts we entertain. We also sin when we fail to do right things. The Bible affirms our own experience— "there is no one righteous, not even one" (Romans 3:10). No matter how good we try to be, none of us does right things all the time.

People tend to divide themselves into groups—good people and bad people. But God says every person who has ever lived is a sinner, and any sin separates us from God. No matter how we might classify ourselves, this includes you and me. We are all sinners.

For all have sinned and fall short of the glory of God.

—Romans 3:23

Many people are confused about the way to God. Some think they will be punished or rewarded according to how good they are. Some think they should make things right in their lives before they try to come to God. Others find it hard to understand how Jesus could love them when other people don't seem to. But I have great news for you! God *does* love you! More than you can ever imagine! And there's nothing you can do to make Him stop! Yes, our sins demand punishment—the punishment of death and separation from God. But because of His great love, God sent His only Son Jesus to die for our sins.

> But God demonstrates his own love for us in this: While we were still sinners, Christ died for us.
>
> —Romans 5:8

For you to come to God, you have to get rid of your sin problem. But not one of us can do this in our own strength! You can't make yourself right with God by being a better person. Only God can rescue us from our sins. He is willing to do this not because of anything you can offer Him, but *just because He loves you!*

> He saved us, not because of righteous things we had done, but because of His mercy.
>
> —Titus 3:5

It's God's grace that allows you to come to Him—not your efforts to "clean up your life" or work your way to heaven. You can't earn it. It's a free gift.

> For it is by grace you have been saved, through faith—and this is not from yourselves, it is the gift of God—not by works, so that no one can boast.

> —Ephesians 2:8–9

For you to come to God, the penalty for your sin must be paid. God's gift to you is His Son Jesus, who paid the debt for you when He died on the Cross.

> For the wages of sin is death, but the gift of God is eternal life in Christ Jesus our Lord.

> —Romans 6:23

Jesus paid the price for your sin and mine by giving His life on a Cross at a place called Calvary, just outside of the city walls of Jerusalem in ancient Israel. God brought Jesus back from the dead. He provided the way for you to have a personal relationship with Him through Jesus. When we realize how deeply our sin grieves the heart of God and how desperately we need a Savior, we are ready to receive God's offer of salvation. To admit we are sinners means turning away from our sin and selfishness and turning to follow Jesus. The Bible's word for this is *repentance*—to change our thinking about how grievous sin is, so our thinking is in line with God's.

All that's left for you to do is to accept the gift that Jesus is holding out for you right now.

> If you declare with your mouth, "Jesus is Lord," and
> believe in your heart that God raised him from the
> dead, you will be saved. For it is with your heart
> that you believe and are justified, and it is with your
> mouth that you profess your faith and are saved.
>
> —Romans 10:9–10

God says that if you believe in His Son Jesus, you can live forever with Him in glory.

> For God so loved the world that He gave his one
> and only Son, that whoever believes in him shall
> not perish but have eternal life.
>
> —John 3:16

Are you ready to accept the gift of eternal life Jesus is offering
you right now? Let's review what this commitment involves:

- I acknowledge I am a sinner in need of a Savior—this is
  to repent or turn away from sin.
- I believe in my heart that God raised Jesus from the
  dead—this is to trust that Jesus paid the full penalty
  for my sins.
- I confess Jesus as my Lord and my God—this is to sur-
  render control of my life to Jesus.
- I receive Jesus as my Savior forever—this is to
  accept that God has done for me and in me what He
  promised.

If it is your sincere desire to receive Jesus into your heart as your personal Lord and Savior, then talk to God from your heart.

Here's a suggested prayer:

"Lord Jesus, I know I am a sinner, and I do not deserve eternal life. But I believe You died and rose from the grave to make me a new creation and to prepare me to dwell in Your presence forever. Jesus, come into my life, take control of my life, forgive my sins, and save me. I am now placing my trust in You alone for my salvation, and I accept your free gift of eternal life. Amen."

How to Share Your Faith

When engaging someone with the gospel, we use the same approach we see Jesus using in Scripture: love, listen, discern, and respond.

Love
Love comes from God
Go out of your way
Go be amongst the crowd
Change your environment

Listen
Ask questions
Listen for the heart issue
Don't defend or argue

Discern

Discernment is from the Holy Spirit
Discern the Holy Spirit's leading
What's the point of entry?

Respond

When we love, listen, and discern, we are prepared to respond, the Holy Spirit does the work, and God is glorified.

Ask, "Is there anything keeping you from accepting the free gift of life in Jesus today?"

You can help your friend pray to receive salvation by praying the prayer on page 68.

How to Pray for Your Friends

For God so loved the world, and that includes the kid in school no one wants to be friends with. If you see someone friendless, say this prayer for them, and then go talk to them about God's love!

God, You came to earth out of love for _____. Loving God, show them Your love today. Help them experience the warmth of knowing You are with them and You love them no matter what.

We are made for relationship. The most important relationship is the one we have with God. We are made to be in relationship with our families too. Sometimes families are not connected in the loving way God intended. If you or your friend struggle with feeling loved by your family, tell God.

God, sometimes families don't show love the way people want or need them to. Just because families don't know how to show love or are not loving us the way we feel like they should, doesn't mean we aren't loved. Open our eyes so we can see the little acts of love our families do show for us. God, help us to love our difficult families the way You want us to.

Sometimes in order to feel loved, we need to show love to others. It's often hard to feel as though we are loved and connected to people when our focus is always on ourselves. If you or a friend struggles to feel loved and connected with friends, tell God how you feel.

God, I don't feel truly loved or connected at school/church/club, etc. I think sometimes my focus is wrong. Instead of trying to love others I'm focused on how alone and unloved I feel. Open a door today/tomorrow for me to focus on loving others. Show me someone who needs an act of kindness done for them, and then give me courage to do it.

God, I don't think _____ feels loved or connected. I think they have put up a wall as a way to protect themselves from hurt. Will you break down their wall so they can experience Your love? Will You help them find the right group to belong to?

**If you enjoyed this book, will you consider
sharing the message with others?**

Let us know your thoughts at info@newhopepublishers.com.
You can also let the author know by visiting or sharing a photo of
the cover on our social media pages or leaving a review
at a retailer's site. All of it helps us get the message out!

Twitter.com/NewHopeBooks
Facebook.com/NewHopePublishers
Instagram.com/NewHopePublishers

New Hope® Publishers is an imprint of Iron Stream Media,
which derives its name from Proverbs 27:17,
"As iron sharpens iron, so one person sharpens another."

This sharpening describes the process of discipleship, one to
another. With this in mind, Iron Stream Media provides a variety
of solutions for churches, missionaries, and nonprofits ranging
from in-depth Bible study curriculum and Christian book publishing to custom publishing and consultative services. Through the
popular Life Bible Study and Student Life Bible Study brands, ISM
provides web-based full-year and short-term Bible study
teaching plans as well as printed devotionals, Bibles,
and discipleship curriculum.

For more information on ISM and
New Hope Publishers, please visit
IronStreamMedia.com
NewHopePublishers.com

Printed in the United States
By Bookmasters